THE IMPORTANCE
OF WONDER

AUTHOR BEN ROBINSON PERFORMING WONDER AT THE RUBIN MUSEUM

DEDICATI°N

This small book is gratefully dedicated to the individuals who found a broken illusionist before them and repaired him with their expertise, and gleeful sense of wondrous resurrection:

Dr. Jason Kendler
Dr. Carl J. Vaughan
Dr. Sudhir Diwan
Dr. Elisabeth Lachmann
Dr. Robert Campagna
Dr. Neel Mehta
Dr. Meredith Lash
Dr. Paul Basuk
Dr. Andrew Weiland
Dr. Michael Sein

Mr. Hector Mayo, PT
Ms. Alexandra MacKenzie, PT
Ms. Jessica Walter, MS, L.Ac
Ms. Cynthia Sablon, MS, L.Ac
Ms. Liza Pollock, MS, L.Ac
Ms. Sarah Sajdak, MS, L.Ac

CONTENTS

PUBLISHER'S NOTE

Several years ago I decided to start the very first free on-line magazine devoted to magicians and variety entertainment. It is called *VANISH* (the International Magic Magazine). We quickly rose to having a solid subscribership of over 100,000 readers in 90 countries. As a full time professional magician, I have spent many years traveling on cruise ships, performing my routines in large theatres afloat. I mention this because I know who is out there in the more than 100 countries I have visited. I speak to them. I correspond with a very few. It would seem idyllic to travel the world, and get paid for entertaining millions of people live. So much so that I wrote a guide to entertaining on cruise ships that has now gone through several editions. I wrote this so I did not have to constantly respond to, or turn down the many who wanted to know who, what, where, and in some cases, why.

During my travels and writing, I encountered a magician based in New York City, whom I quickly realized could really write. It is said that anyone can write, but few have something to say. Luckily for me and the readers of *VANISH* Ben Robinson also has something very important to say.

I've implored Ben to write for my blog, for my books and then was persistent to have him join *VANISH* first as a (frequent) contributor, and now as a Contributing Editor.

Then came his submission of The Importance of Wonder. I had forgotten we began discussing the topic sometime in 2012 when he was finishing a show at New York City's famed Museum of the Moving Image where he not only consulted on the overall program titled MAGICIANS ON SCREEN, but presented the gala stage show in the spectacular theatre, complete with original props used in the movies from 1896 to 2011. What impressed me, however, was his lecture-presentation titled Magic &The Silent Clowns, which became the largest attended non-celebrity event in the Museum's history, and also a book (by the same title) that quickly sold out its initial edition. The overall show came about because of the Martin Scorsese film HUGO, based on the life of magician-film pioneer Georges Melies. Ben and I agreed that "wonder" was central to the silent clowns' success, and the overall impression of HUGO, but that wonder was the essential component in a successful magician's performance. As we continued the discussion, I realized he really had something to say.

The Importance of Wonder was serialized in *VANISH* from December 2014 through May 2015. This is the first time the magazine has ever published an article as a stand-alone piece. We are very proud to have Jim Steinmeyer along for this gripping exploration of the magician's central cause. As well, we are very grateful to Executive Director Erica Stone of the American Himalayan Foundation for allowing us to print the cover shot by Ben, which he donated to their Foundation in 1991 for their use to raise funds benefitting the Sherpa population in the great Solo Khumbu, Nepal.

You will read in the Afterword how this amazing photograph came to be. Jim Steinmeyer's Foreword has deeply insightful thoughts on why wonder is important. Then we'll part the curtain and let Mr. Robinson take the stage. Were the word not overused, dare I say, you are in for a wondrous experience.

—*Paul Romhany*
Editor-in-Chief
VANISH International Magic Magazine
Vancouver, BC
February 2015
www.vanishmagazine.com

FOREWORD

Alas!

We are no longer dumbstruck or enchanted by the thoughts of a "thinking machine!" The Georgians or Victorians introduced the possibility of these devices, turning them into quaint totems of foreign mystery, adorned with the carved wooden heads of a sly "Turk" or a mysterious dark "Hindoo." Those were de Kempelen's famous chess playing automata or Maskelyne's whist-playing Psycho, both tricks to deceive and delight their audiences with whispers of technology, concealed within great gales of blustery showmanship. Today we hold real "thinking machines" in the palm of our hands. They talk to us, give us directions, and offer instant connections to other people. Their sleek, cold lack of personality is part of their appeal. We use them, in part, because we no longer need to marvel over them. And they provide a fraction of the wonders of The Turk or Psycho.

The inevitable march of technology has been, through the twentieth century, a continual familiarization with marvels. The pace of technology has been insured by our ability to shake hands with marvels within weeks of their introductions. For about a hundred years, the western world found it necessary to hold "World's Fairs," grand celebrations to introduce new cultures, new thoughts, and new technology to the masses. It was at the World's Fairs that society first met the telephone, phonograph, and electric light—standing within a crowd of onlookers, to marvel and admire. Those World's Fairs moved too slowly for modern technology, and went the way of vaudeville, the telegraph, the steam locomotive. Today, the DSL cable that arrives at our desktop supplants the ticket to a World's Fair. We read about a new idea, see it demonstrated, just hours after the inventor held it in his hands. We are no longer part of a crowd of onlookers. We share our morning coffee with the latest ideas. There is no time to marvel; we are told to quickly meet and shake hands with the things that used to leave us awestruck.

And whither wonder?

Has the march of technology really been an active extermination of the emotion of wonder? In many ways, it is the magician who can best provide an "honest" (and yes, the word applies with a certain irony) experience of wonder, tied tightly to current culture, echoing timeless traditions, and adorned with the trappings of popular entertainment. It is the magician who can best turn an entertainment experience into a real marvel.

But one of the great ironies of the magician's art is that magicians seem too embarrassed, too confused, or too unsure of themselves to understand this need for wonder. It's a word that magicians seldom use, somehow associating it with the "airy-fairy" aspirations of the New Age. My friend Ben Robinson and I had the pleasure of knowing and working with the late Doug Henning, who used the word without prejudice; Doug always understood this goal and spoke cogently about the emotion. It formed his philosophy of magic, and it was a philosophy that seemed to embarrass the hard-nosed magicians of his generation.

I'm delighted that Ben Robinson's fascinating, stream of consciousness essay on wonder will find a new audience in this book. It's a subject he is uniquely qualified to discuss; it's a subject I've heard him return to in some of our most memorable conversations.

Today, when your fellow magicians are unsure of themselves— it is a profession that's unappreciated and often neglected— they take cover by cloaking themselves in the guise of something more popular. They joke through their performances in the style of stand-up comedy; they shrug about the goofy, dorky appeal of magic, attempting to sidle up the audience with self-effacing humor. Just tricks. It's not really about doing magic, it's all about your personality, after all. Just deliver a show, and take a check.

Somewhere, right now, a mediocre artist is standing at a canvas, blobbing paint onto the surface as efficiently as he can. This will be one of the "works of art" that will hang in a hotel room. The paint is applied quickly, according to a formula, to produce something that reminds us of the real thing. "Art?" the painter might tell you with cheery, self-effacing honesty. "Hey, buddy, this isn't art. All I'm doing is putting down paint to produce a product, to make a few bucks." We might be suspicious of a man standing at an easel who won't talk about art.

Similarly, we might be suspicious of a magician standing on a stage who won't talk about wonder.

It is not an ultimate aspiration. It is the only aspiration. It is the mark of a real magician. It is the necessary job, the unquestionable goal, and, as Ben Robinson quite simply and courageously insists, for centuries it has remained our compass bearing, whether we wish to realize it or not.

—*Jim Steinmeyer*
November 26, 2014

Jim Steinmeyer has been called "the most influential non-performing magician in history." He has designed illusions for A-list magicians such as Siegfried & Roy, Doug Henning and Lance Burton. For Ringling Bros. circus he designed the method by which an elephant vanished while completely surrounded in arenas across the US. Currently on Broadway, he is the mastermind behind Disney's flying carpet in the smash hit musical *Aladdin*. He has written over 20 books on the subject as well as treatises on the origins of Dracula, Charles Fort and the science behind the 19th century's most striking illusion, Pepper's Ghost. He lives in Burbank, CA with his producer wife Frankie Glass. www.jimsteinmeyer.com.

about the goofy, dorky appeal of magic, attempting to sidle up the audience with self-effacing humor. Just tricks. It's not really about doing magic, it's all about your personality, after all. Just deliver a show, and take a check.

Somewhere, right now, a mediocre artist is standing at a canvas, blobbing paint onto the surface as efficiently as he can. This will be one of the "works of art" that will hang in a hotel room. The paint is applied quickly, according to a formula, to produce something that reminds us of the real thing. "Art?" the painter might tell you with cheery, self-effacing honesty. "Hey, buddy, this isn't art. All I'm doing is putting down paint to produce a product, to make a few bucks." We might be suspicious of a man standing at an easel who won't talk about art.

Similarly, we might be suspicious of a magician standing on a stage who won't talk about wonder.

It is not an ultimate aspiration. It is the only aspiration. It is the mark of a real magician. It is the necessary job, the unquestionable goal, and, as Ben Robinson quite simply and courageously insists, for centuries it has remained our compass bearing, whether we wish to realize it or not.

—*Jim Steinmeyer*
November 26, 2014

Jim Steinmeyer has been called "the most influential non-performing magician in history." He has designed illusions for A-list magicians such as Siegfried & Roy, Doug Henning and Lance Burton. For Ringling Bros. circus he designed the method by which an elephant vanished while completely surrounded in arenas across the US. Currently on Broadway, he is the mastermind behind Disney's flying carpet in the smash hit musical *Aladdin*. He has written over 20 books on the subject as well as treatises on the origins of Dracula, Charles Fort and the science behind the 19th century's most striking illusion, Pepper's Ghost. He lives in Burbank, CA with his producer wife Frankie Glass. www.jimsteinmeyer.com.

THE IMPORTANCE OF WONDER

(Enter Ghost. He resembles the recently deceased King of Denmark, Hamlet Sr.)

Marcellus: Peace, break thee off; look, where it comes again!
Bernardo: In the same figure, like the king that's dead.
Marcellus: Thou art a scholar; speak to it, Horatio.
Bernardo: Looks it not like the king? Mark it, Horatio.
Horatio: Most like; it harrows me with fear and wonder.

—from Tragedy of HAMLET, Prince of Denmark by William Shakespeare, Act I. Scene 1. p. 43. 1888 edition. Tragedy of HAMLET, Prince of Denmark was written in 1504 (first known Parisian edition printed 1514).

The Entertainment Director of the world famous Magic Castle in Hollywood, CA is named Jack Goldfinger, a very accomplished magician himself. Mr. Goldfinger told me when he booked me to appear at the famed private club, "When I inherited this job, I was given a rolodex with 2,000 magician's names in it." The Magic Castle books roughly ten magicians weekly, which, if you do the math, given they are open almost 365 days a year, is 520 magicians' performances yearly. It is an amazing statistic. Given that the Egyptian Hall of London, England survived presenting magicians, first under the aegis of John Nevil Maskelyne, and later his partner, Britain's greatest magician, David Devant, for sixty years (1873—1933), the Magic Castle is quickly approaching the same status nearly100 years later.

The Magic Castle is an institution unlike any other, and while challenged to survive in rough economy, and endured a devastating fire that broke out a few Halloweens ago, it is a sure barometer for the "state of magic." (Over 120 firemen responded to the call when fire broke out surely edifying the city's love of the famed bastion of all things magical.) It would seem that the Magic Castle is perfectly situated to be the Mecca of all magicdom, and has sustained its position because it provides magic as it was meant to be seen; entertainment that provides an audience with good feeling about themselves and provides a genuinely wondrous experience, clearly demonstrated in the exclamation by patrons, "How did that happen?"

Do all of the magicians who appear at the Magic Castle elicit this feeling?

> *"In conjuring the emphasis is—or should be—on the mysterious, wonderful and illusory aspects of the presentation."*
> *—S. H. Sharpe, Words on Wonder*

You may see magicians on TV. And someone not familiar with magicians in general may think that the "number one magician" (whatever that really means) is therefore the best.

(A viral video may provide that famous 15-minutes for a newbie magician which today magician Rory Feldman, a giant Thurston collector, says "is more like fifteen seconds." Mr. Feldman has a point.)

FAME TODAY

What does "the best" mean today? Who is the "most famous" magician? In Thurston's day (Thurston lived from 1869 – 1936), he explained in many interviews that the "best magician was the one with the best (most copious) advertising." However, Thurston was also quick to counsel younger magicians that the "world's greatest magician *ceased* to be the greatest if they started to believe their own press." There is the rub. (Thurston knew, as purveyor of his massive 3-train car, 40-person cast, traveling *Wonder Show of the Universe,* that, as writers create fiction for the page, magicians' illusions were only for the stage. If greatness is selfless, then it should remain on the stage. Off stage bombastic ego is boring and potentially abusive.)

So, ask yourself, right now, today, is the best magician the most famous?

> *"In the future everybody will be*
> *famous for fifteen minutes."*
> *—Andy Warhol*

Fame itself, has changed. Attention spans have changed. Both have been affected by the "prosthesis" of technology, roughly beginning in the 1880's with the industrialization of the planet Earth. When Columbus' boats sailed from Spain, Queen Isabella invoked a holy prayer asking God for protection of the ships she patronized. When the steam engine came into being, God had little to do with safe passage, or perhaps, not as much, compared to the smooth running of the steam-powered vessel.

A hundred years ago, or more, in Maskelyne, Devant or Thurston's day, one *actually had to do something* to become famous. The model for theatrical success of the 19th century was simple, but hard to do: learn your lessons (go to dance class); then, perform as much as possible, in increasingly better venues—from local dance recitals to national competitions. Then, you prepared yourself so chance could favor "your shot." If you felt prepared, the day Mr. Spielberg would be in your audience and wanted you for his next film, would be the day you'd planned for most of your adult life.

In 2015, "the game" has changed radically, and there has been devastating "collateral damage"—to use a term of modern warfare. It seems that while someone who has a lot of money may become famous for having a huge amount of cash (but little else) or for having had sex on the Internet, these factors are quickly becoming common place, and it is no longer surprising or shocking for the populace at large to realize that (insert your favorite famous name) has either a drug problem, smashed up a car or yelled out drunkenly at a Broadway show and then punched a guard.

But, let's be very clear, fame is *not* performance.

Being famous in 2015 is not necessarily the result of talent. In fact, talent has largely taken a backseat to promotion; form becoming the content of the 21st century.

These statements are not meant to depress, or beat up anyone in particular. But, the consequences are depressing and devastating to the general audience of this essay: people who call themselves "magicians."

THE VAUDEVILLIAN EDICT

Few people who performed in Vaudeville are still living. But, I knew a good deal of people who did, and they all agreed on one point: "When it comes to the myth or the truth — the myth, print that!" they yowl.

Given that the myth of Houdini escaping the frozen top of the river in Detroit has become lore, the blurring of lines of a magician's performance take on added dimension. No, Houdini was never under the ice, and his own brother, Theodore Weiss (29 February 1876 — 12 June 1945), known professionally as "Hardeen," who did his share of bridge jumps nearly naked swathed in chains told a friend of mine that the most difficult part of doing a "challenge bridge jump" was not escaping the locks and chains, under water, "but, not shivering too much in the icy cold and having the chains fall off before you hit the water."

Our point is that magicians live to create myths and that is why people pay to see a magician; audiences *crave* surprise.

Surprise itself is quite lacking in a technologically over run society that promises miracles with a simple click. You want any book? Go to Amazon.com and click. You want a date for the night where sex is assured? That too can be procured if you have the right connections, credit card and security protocols. Nothing surprising about that. It used to be that if you wanted a book, you had to go to a bookstore, and ask, hope or "order." A date was something that came because you met someone at a social place or were introduced via mutual connections.

Today, the computer or smart phone has become the Rosetta Stone of convenience. It has produced the attitude of almost jaded contempt for we who offer wonder-working selflessly, or maybe with self-promotion in mind.

I was saddened and shocked to perform an expert conjuring effect of Emil Jarrow's where a dime disappeared instantaneously and then immediately seemed to penetrate upwards into a shot glass. A woman watching at a party at The Waldorf Astoria hotel remarked, "Yeah, that and a quarter will get you on the subway." She was implying that my work meant little to nothing. It hurt. So much so, twenty years later, I still remember this happening. (BTW, many people looked upon this little feat and were charmed, but I am prone to remember the one snarky comment as opposed to the many smiles.)

THE PROBLEM WITH MAGIC IN 2015

This leaves we who conjure with common objects with a problem. When you can zap up any performance of U2, Frank Sinatra or The Cleveland Orchestra on any video channel, and sit home dressed as you wish, you don't have to buy a ticket and wonder if the person in front of you will be too tall, smelly or obnoxiously blocking your view you paid hundreds to see.

The problem for magicians is that magic, to be successful, must exist in the same time and space as the audience. Briefly, let us offer a definition of "success." It would seem, that if we call ourselves "magicians" then it would follow that our actions should be "magical" in some context. While differing cultures might view "magic" as either "that which is impossible (or, unlikely)" it is my suspicion that being magical entails something positively charming, while the nature of magic being outside of most people's actions is what separates magicians from non-magicians. Magicians, therefore, can do something others cannot!

However, the devil is in the details. It is my sole opinion that "successful magic" is also that which entertains with unusual creativity. To be blunt: If the audience has seen it (what you do) before, then I don't think you are doing your job as well as you might.

"But people are curious, and Mr. Baily and I, we like to encourage curiosity, for we have learned long since that curiosity will eventually lead to wonder. And is that not the chiefest occupation of any wizard, but the deliberate provocation of wonder? We think so."
—Professor Gus Rich, portrayed by
Max Howard, in the play *The War Wizard*

Magic, also, must not be confrontational, eliciting Las Vegas' long-running, award-winning comedy magician Mac King's recent comment in the documentary titled *OUR MAGIC* that "Magicians say 'I made that disappear ...bitch.'" It brings the ire of popular comedians like Jerry Seinfeld who quip that magicians aren't magicians, and therefore *not* worth watching ...ouch.

Magicians who had heavily edited TV specials in the 1980's quickly found that once people started buying VCRs and watching the tapes over and over and learned that the special's editing was seen for what it was; selling out an art form to become wealthy. If anyone could edit together a set of highly-controlled, skillfully shot (read specific camera angles that revealed as much as they obscured), then what exactly were major advertisers paying for that included their product in the overall parade?

Why would a big soft drink company "sponsor" outright cheating, when it had previously been the case that when magicians appeared on live TV, magicians were booked and looked upon as not only doing something, but also, doing something *extraordinary*? The audience felt cheated in the end; learning the magicians involved with video editing did not sustain the ethical "agreement" guiding the "willing suspension of disbelief." After all, the magician was a celebrated, often very talented individual who was able to accomplish not just something amazing, but clever, and seemingly had solved problems thought impossible, such as vanishing an elephant (that was away from all curtains, trapdoors and apparatus that could mask the elephant's quick exit).

Many a modern magician has heard in the 21st century while professionally entertaining tableside in restaurants (such as Howie Marmer known as Howie the Great, Atlanta's #1 magician), "I've never seen magic up close. I always thought it was TV editing tricks like that guy on TV." The boots on the ground magicians meet the perception warped by the millionaire marketer performers who flat out "cheat" and deliver unreal expectations for real performers. It's a *real* problem.

BEN ROBINSON CREATING WONDER

IMPOSSIBLE VS. IMPROBABLE

If TV editing were the cause, there was no real magic felt, certainly no artfulness, and definitely no chance for the emotion of wonder to grow and delight the viewer.

Dr. John N. Booth (1912—2009), regarded by many as one of the finest magicians of his day (once filling in for Cardini) titled his final book *Extending Magic Beyond Credibility* (2001). Booth reasoned, as Harry Anderson points out, "Magic is based not on what is impossible, but what is improbable." Wonder was effectively put out of business on American network TV, because TV executives more concerned with "branding" and advertising revenue, accepted the use of electronic means to affect the seemingly miraculous.

Consequently, a generation has grown tired of magicians (in general) because their claims were not only unfounded, lacking any real problem-solving skill, but because their methods held contempt for intelligence. And, with this "model" in place, such magicians provided little wonder. You did not leave your TV-viewing being amazed, but rather disappointed.

Generally, when people are yawning, they are NOT intellectually engaged, much less entertained.

The off-stage contempt for the audience by the narcissism of the TV magicians (hiding their incompetence as performers), who engaged in this contemptible conduct wrought ultimate disregard, if not mutual contempt, by late 20th century audiences.

BEN ROBINSON WITH JOHN BOOTH AND JOHNNY ACE PALMER

DOUG HENNING & WONDER

Doug Henning (1947—2000) achieved enormous fame by having appeared on Broadway, opening in *The Magic Show* May 28, 1974. Following his revolutionary success, from 1975 to 1982 he produced and starred in eight TV specials, the first four presented live with limited commercial interruption. In other words, Henning presented a legitimate stage show. The first special, broadcast December 26, 1975 brought an audience of 50 million viewers— a statistic that has never been duplicated by any other magician.

His first four live specials (done on the NBC-TV network), created a mass of love and respect for the artist and his art because Henning insisted his performance was untainted by zealous camera shots or editing.

Later, when watching a competitor who adopted his yearly model, but craftily used video editing to create astonishing effects, the small, longhaired magician exclaimed to friends, "That guy just ruined all the good will I created with the audience over the last seven years." As broadly recounted in John Harrison's biography of Doug Henning (*SPELLBOUND: The Wonder Filled Life of Doug Henning*), Henning was furious.

In 1982, the pixie illusionist performed on his last TV special, which this writer participated in, however briefly. I saw his exhaustion of creating one final gargantuan TV special that was titled "Doug Henning on Broadway" and was largely a commercial for his forthcoming massive Broadway show titled MERLIN, with some illusions that had never been performed before. (MERLIN was in part financed by Doug's old friend from Canada Ivan Reitman who was able to get Columbia motion pictures to finance the show; at the time, the most expensive Broadway musical—ever.)

In that final TV spectacular, Henning offered a "greatest hits" of his previous seven TV specials and while the show was taped in front of a live audience, the final product the home audience saw, was an edited performance. On his 4th special, tigers involved in one of the concluding effects became untethered and roamed the halls of NBC. That catastrophe put an end to the variables of Henning's live TV ambitions.

The last time I saw Doug he had hired me to "do the pitch" of a tie-in between Revlon products called Color Magic, and his Broadway show MERLIN. As I stood at the Bloomingdale's counter in the center of Manhattan, he watched as I nervously transformed a silk handkerchief into an egg. "Ben, remember, it's all about wonder. If you give that feeling to the audience, we succeed. It's all about wonder. Remember that." He said that and then he left with his small entourage. I never saw him again.

> *"It's all about wonder. Remember that."*
> *—Doug Henning*

Doug espoused his theory of wonder a bit more cogently in print. He wrote in his biography, *HOUDINI—His Legend & His Magic* (1976):

"Magic, that art which has uplifted the minds and hearts of people down through history, creating wonder. Wonder is a very subtle, precious emotion, often lost in the gross hustle and bustle of modern life. When we feel wonder, we are immediately reminded of the purity and innocence of our childhood. Then everything was magical, everything was mysterious."

During an interview with Robert Neubert in *New Realities* magazine, two years later, Doug mentioned:

"Once you feel wonder for the world, your heart starts to expand. It's exactly what I've gone through in my growth. It's what happens in the growth from ignorance to enlightenment. The awe just melts into love, and that's unity."

Today, some snide magicians seem to think that Doug Henning was an atypical, aberration of his times, a post—1960's flower child that danced the light fantastic with rainbows on pink overalls. Those cash-minded hucksters who seem to think money is the end all, forget that in 1979, Doug Henning was offered half-a-million dollars a week for his performance in Las Vegas, and he turned it down.

The art, science, philosophy of the magician's performance is about one thing and one thing only: *inspiring the fragile emotion of wonder*. Without the end result of a magician making the audience "ooh and ahh," the "magician" is merely a self-critical buffoon, or someone pleasing themselves with others' hands (and dollars).

It's tough talk, but it has to be said, the state of magic, disregarded by arts councils who give grants to actors, writers, painters, dancers and "performance artists" do not regard magicians as "artists." The reason is because certain TV magicians of the 1980's and 1990's perverted the trust built by magicians like Doug Henning, Mark Wilson, and Milbourne Christopher—none of whom relied on video editing to make magic a palatable entertainment for the masses.

DOUG HENNING IN THE MAGIC SHOW.
PHOTO COURTESY OF DOUG HENNING.

THE ASTAIRE EXAMPLE

In late 2014, the celebrated pianist Michael Feinstein gave a video tribute to Fred Astaire widely seen on the Turner Classic Movies channel. Amidst the moments of praise and career highlights, Feinstein noted that Astaire not only was the first to tell a story through his dance, but he was always pushing the boundaries of his profession. Because of this, film was a natural medium. Astaire was seen as dancing with an animated chorus line of disembodied shoes, and once he even defied gravity and danced up a wall and onto the ceiling.

However, Fred Astaire realized one extremely important point: he never let his technological showmanship interfere with his seemingly effortless dance technique. He was exacting and forthright to make damn sure that his dance was recorded in wide single camera shots, only edited together for an occasional close up. Fred Astaire wanted to keep the trust with his audience that he was one of the world's greatest dancers. To rely on filmic gimmickry would be a slap in the face to those who had paid to see him.

If certain TV magicians had only the intelligence to understand the genius of Fred Astaire and his methodology! You don't have to be a genius to appreciate genius. Magic suffers to be recognized as an art because the art was sold out as cheap and unremarkable by those who simply did not care using the TV medium.

A pro delivers wonder, period. For the pro; if you don't *really* deliver, then, well, you don't eat. It's that simple. Therefore, what is "delivering?" The answer may be found in history.

MONTAUK MANOR, NY (2006—2012)

MALINI & MYTH

It may be a myth that Max Malini (1872—1942) was engaged at a wealthy woman's house in the US, where he asked for a small table to perform his blindfolded card stabbing feat (well seen and duplicated on Paul Daniels' DVD *Malini the Magician*, a live recording of his performance in London's West End). The greatest part of the myth being, that when Malini plunged the knife down on the table to stab the card, the hostess exclaimed in horror that Malini had put a knife mark into the expensive table. The hostess is to have screamed "Sir, you just put a huge gash in a Louis the XVIth table!"

Malini allegedly replied, "Ma'am, You may tell everyone Malini did it."

Who knows if the story is true? But, it's a good story and has all the hallmarks of the life little, fat, audacious Malini lived. Malini's business card read:

MALINI

You'll wonder when I am coming.
You'll wonder more when I am gone.

MALINI ADVERT 1914

Malini understood, and created wonder. This is why he is truly legendary, in the very definition of the word "legendary." Few magicians in history have the resume of Malini's of entertaining as many monarchs and world leaders. Just what did the most powerful men and women in the world seek in the magician Malini when they had all the money and power the world could offer? I believe that wealth and influence sought something outside of their sphere; ergo, wonder. To me this is the only reasonable answer —monarchs and Presidents sought another kind of power—the power of magic.

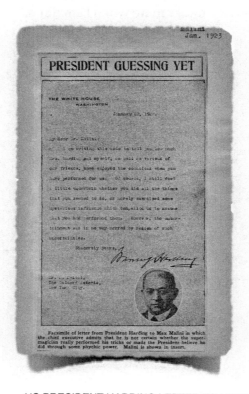

US PRESIDENT HARDING LETTER TO MALINI

Having featured a card stab for most of my career (being given a great piece of material by my magic teacher Milbourne Christopher [1914—1984] as my college graduation present in 1981), I can confirm the power of a wondrous piece of magic that has a beginning, middle and dramatic conclusion. I am proud to report that my card stab has been called "the best in the business" by magicians, audiences and critics from Stockbridge, MA, to Las Vegas to Kiev, Russia. I mention that because magicians are lucky to be identified with a single illusion the way Frank Sinatra is aligned with the song (written by Paul Anka) *My Way,* or Bob Hope having a theme song played when he entered or exited, *Thanks For The Memories.*

BEN ROBINSON'S CARD STAB - PHOTO: KEVIN THOMASSON

Having very personal material is a distinction between not just professionals and amateurs, but between an entertainer who considers their "temporary market" and an artist investing in a life's work. I am the latter.

I don't think of myself in any active sense as a philosopher, but it is certainly true that I am given, and for long years have been given, to that part of the philosophical process called wonder. Wonder, I think, begins with simple curiosity and some form of marveling, leading inevitably to the asking of that vital question, "Why?" and all this in hope that some solid answers might supply themselves. I find that I am doing that increasingly in my life, and in taking my great concern for the land and assessing that concern, I ask, many questions. Oftener than not, I find no answers other than this: many people are indescribably wanton in their despoilation of the

31

*land either through stupidity or a colossal selfishness—and I use
"colossal" in its true or non-Hollywood sense.*

—James Cagney
Cagney By Cagney (1976)

**AMERICAN MAGICIAN JOHN
MULHOLLAND WITH THE SULTAN
OF SULU, 1920'S.**

*"He (John Mulholland) agreed
and went on with the usual
rigmarole of making things
disappear and reappear, and
then turned to the Sultan with
the remark 'I can't possibly
understand why money should
be so scarce in Jolo when even
the air is full of it.'
He thereupon took off his coat,
rolled up his sleeves, and pulled
silver dollars out of the air until
the floor was littered with them.
The Sultan's eyes popped so far
out of his head that they could
have been knocked off with a
stick. To think that the air was so full of money and he who
needed it so much had not been able to discover it. He was
inarticulate with amazement, and I do not know to this day, what
he really thought of the performance."*
—Dr. Victor Heiser
An American Doctor's Odyssey—Adventures in Forty-five Countries,
W.W. Norton & Company, Inc., 1936. P.148-149.

In 1981 I attended the Simon & Garfunkel Reunion Concert in Central Park along with 500,000 other people who came to the free show. Most of us who wanted to be within one hundred yards of the stage arrived early that morning. I spent a good part of the day defending my turf and doing magic for people. I featured my card stab.

Five years later, I was featured at an opium den-like "bar" in Paris called *Casablanca's* and began work at midnight and stopped my strolling table-side magic at 4am. I usually left my friend Bruno's apartment on the Left Bank of the Siene at 10:30pm to arrive early, set my props, have a drink at the bar, warm up and then hit it at midnight, and work non-stop until 4am. One night I was walking along Rue Quixcompais and a man stopped me. It was unnerving.

"Êtes-vous le magicien?" he asked.

"Oui" I replied. I thought he had seen me at the club as, I was featured for one week and it was in the middle of the week.

He then dug into his carrying bag and produced his wallet. From within he pulled out a tattered Nine of Hearts playing card with an even more tattered hole in the center. The Frenchman then explained he had seen me at the Simon & Garfunkel concert five years earlier. Then he told me that he had been trying to figure out my magic since that time. He continued that he *always* carried the stabbed, revealed card, to tell other people of my performance; and get their reaction. (He also added that this was a great pick-up story for women!)

> ***"Magic has to be believed to be seen."***
> —Harry Anderson

Harry Anderson used to say in interviews: "Magic has to be believed to be seen." I agree with my friend Harry. In fact, the proof of the pudding is this: Dunninger used to read minds over the radio and get high ratings, huge compliments and yearly renewed contracts by huge sponsors like the US Steel Company. Another kind of magic, ventriloquism, often thought to be impossible to deliver over the radio was done very successfully for many years by Edgar Bergen and his clever ventriloquil figure sidekick, Charlie McCarthy.

Magic has to be believed to be seen (or in this case, heard). Magic has to be simple to be understood.

HARRY ANDERSON FROM A SCENE IN NIGHT COURT 1986 - PHOTO: COURTESY NBC-TV

A veteran performer, Charles Windley, was nine years old, when he first saw a feat of magic. A bus driver, who took him to school, cut and restored a single strand of rope. Windley went on in a career spanning 65-years to become one of the famous mainstays of Hubert's Museum in the Times Square area. He is also one of the attractions made immortal having been photographed by the famous photographer Diane Arbus. Windley is a performer who has seen and done it all. He knows that his job has always been about producing wonder for audiences. Windley laments, "Today, magicians have no idea what they are supposed to be doing."

The feat he saw (the cut and restored rope) is genuinely legendary, probably originating over a thousand years ago. The rope is shown to be whole, ungimmicked. It is then severed into two pieces. Finally, because of magical powers it is restored into one whole piece again. Simple; to see, understand, and in some cases, to perform.

(The power of this effect was such that one of the most influential magicians in history, John Mulholland (1898—1970) claimed that while large circulation magazine pieces he wrote, or was featured in, failed to get him work; once having done the cut and restored rope at a party brought him a thousand dollar fee for performing this one feat (in 1939). What was it that the audience was so desperate to see Mulholland perform, that they would part with one thousand dollars (in today's currency this is the equivalent of $5,000)? I believe the audience craved the feeling this miracle produces: wonder.)

In his travels, Windley found himself with a broken down car in the middle of Virginia late one night. He was taken in by a farmer who took pity on the broken down vehicle carrying the magician and his family. The farmer explained that Windley was only the second magician he had ever seen, Thurston being the first during the Depression. Then the farmer left the room and returned with the family Bible. At the time of the telling of the tale to Windley, the 1960's, this Bible was over 150-years old. A sacred object to this family, handed down through generations.

"I thought he was going to engage us all in prayer" Windley remembers.

The farmer then spoke of witnessing Thurston's show, when the farmer was a small boy. "And do you know what he did? He made a tree grow from a pot and then bloom roses! He then cut off the blooms and tossed them into the audience. See? Here!"

Windley then relates that the farmer opened the Bible and in the center was a blackened, but perfectly preserved rose bloom.This is the power that *wonder-producing* Magic has. It is not to be underestimated.

WINDLEY PERFORMS THE SUBSTITUTION TRUNK

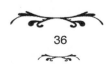

SUNKEN SHIPS

People who angrily criticize all magicians, or worse, magicians who utter lines like: "Whadya think I'm a damn magician for God's sake?" not only lack creativity, but they do a disservice to all magicians. They lack wonder. They sink the ship before it even sails.

Of course, magicians must take the helm and steer their ship to the wondrous. They must first ask the hard questions: What is magic? What is a magician? Why am I making this bowl of water disappear? What is wonder? Ask yourself. Do you know? If you don't, you have no business stepping on stage calling yourself a magician, illusionist or conjuror.

Do you just want to be famous, rich, or have lots of sex? Or, do you want to inspire wonder, give an uplifting feeling…or genuinely entertain? Who are you trying to please? The audience or yourself? I think if your answer is "both" you are on the right track.

If you do the hard work, and write down your acts as a script including stage directions[1] or in the case of a table-top performance, where the props go before the show, and after they are used, and how long the reactions are likely to be, then the magician will begin to learn that: A) The Art of Magic is an offshoot of the theatre at large, and B) there is far more to be

---

[1] See: Max Howard, *Creating Theatrical Magic,* Theory and Art of Magic Press, 2014.

gained by telling a wonder-filled story that will have the positive reaction of the audience feeling good about themselves, but also, feeling good about magicians.

Having followed this theory on stages in 22 countries, in over 10,000 performances, has brought me repeat bookings, sometimes as much as 25 years later. I am convinced that my audiences dig my brand of wonder-based entertainment and verily crave the raw emotion I have learned to provide.

The outright contempt popular comedians and other entertainers have had for magicians are understandable in a society where everything is disposable. Those who don't do their homework (asking the necessary questions regarding this responsibility as performers of *m-a-g-i-c*) before stepping in front of an audience are literally asking for ridicule.

But the harm goes much further. We live in a society where most everything is obtainable, therefore disposable; therefore valued less and less.

Magic, by its very nature, should be special. This does not just apply to young audiences.

An elderly man on his deathbed in New York City once requested my services as the last thing he'd see on Earth. His son called me with the gravity of the situation. I'd only met this man once before, ten years earlier. I was told I could write my own ticket; charge whatever I desired; no price too high. Unfortunately, I did not get there in time and the man died, his wish unfulfilled.

Doing magic properly is great fun, but also a great responsibility. A special responsibility. *Really* special.

CREATING WONDER

It is an open debate: can one deliver wonder if you have *never* personally felt wonder?

I've often contended that the so-called magician MUST imbibe, ingest, consume or inhabit a spoonful of the metaphysical in order to deliver it to a paying audience. Therefore a definition of "metaphysical" might be in order.

meta·phys·i·cal *adjective* \-'fi-zi-kəl\
: of, relating to, or based on metaphysics
: of or relating to things that are thought to exist but that cannot be seen

(Many sources claim "metaphysics" is *not* an easy term to define!)

It doesn't matter how you get to experience genuine wonder. Whether it be organized religion, sexual ecstasy, or an organic hallucinogenic—we recommend nothing. We recommend you think about this. We recommend you consider what you are doing is not tricks, or puzzles that simply confound.

The magicians' job is to entertain through providing a romp into visual, almost liquescent and metamorphic fiction; a poetic foray into the transcendental. One good exercise is to ponder, at least for ten minutes, the differences—if there are any—between "eternity" and "the infinite." If you can expand your mind with this exercise, you may be well on your way to knowing something the other fellow does not. People may pay you for your unique understanding if you can convey your understanding in an artful way.

Consider the Sistine Chapel ceiling. How did Michelangelo achieve painting with the perspective of hundreds of feet of distance while he lay on his back on a scaffolding inches from the surface he painted? Do you wonder? Can you explain the miracle of his chipping away from a massive marble slab all that was not his sculpture named "David" as the artist claimed?

Michelangelo's achievements — wondrous. Genuinely wondrous. To create, produce, perpetrate and incite the miraculous, engendering wonder takes skill achieved through serious work. Be ready to fail, and absorb the lessons. This is not work for the meek.

Don't let your lack of education beat up, or take down an art form. It has become the parlance of popular entertainment to ridicule, known as "riffing." This has its place when the target is not sacred. Killing the Easter Bunny or telling a child they are stupid because they believe in Santa Claus is akin to setting a church on fire, in my opinion. Cynical ridicule burns wondrous belief; life-sustaining, hope-inducing faith. In faith there is hope.

It is not blind faith because wonder is real. Wonder creates ideas. Wonder is the stuff that beckons progress of humans. It may be that wonder is the only thing that can save the human animal. Why? Because wonder incites creativity and solutions. The imagination is fired to extreme possibilities unrecognized prior.

Take the time to learn what magic is; what a magic show should and can be. Doing something well is much harder than just phoning it in. But, it is also much more rewarding to do something that has never been done before (or, as you perform the effect).

It is cheap, nasty, spiteful and largely illiterate to damn "all magicians" for the mistakes of the amateur who is largely just satisfying their own ego. "I can do this and you can't" is a mindset that has no place in the work of creating illusions of "magic" and creating wonder in the audience.

A psychologist of some note, a former Chief Resident of Neuro-Anesthesia at Mount Sinai Hospital (for fifteen years), Dr. John Ryder, once said to me, "Ben, do shows, make money, be happy." I was angered he'd reduced my anxieties to a simple six words. I later wrought great comfort in his distillation. It is also true that it has taken me the forty years I've been a full time traveling professional magician to appreciate the damage done by those who phone it in (largely on TV) through means not offered in the texts that teach "classic magic." That is, *the magic of the masters of an art form for over one hundred years*. I hope you read that sentence over again.

It seems, modern show biz and classic magic—largely developed after Robert-Houdin (1805—1871), have little in common. TV is a voracious medium that produces voluminous mediocrity. Magic is an art that provides one with the ability to develop a "good nine minutes" over a lifetime. I don't think magic works on TV except to be a commercial for a live show.

Sam Sharpe, known by some as the "Aldous Huxley of Magic," a good friend of mine, whose home I visited in Bridlington, England in 1986, wrote to me in a letter, "Ben, as you travel in your career as a thaumaturge (Ed.—arcaic word for magician), you will find that the general feeling by those in the craft at large find the theoretical aspect of magic for cranks and those that like to amuse themselves with abstractions. They feel the notion of wonder and genuine wonderworking, as you seek to do, has little relevance to modern conjuring or popular entertainment. Especially when you are going up against the other guy in hard-nosed business; they who have little patience for 'artistry.'" Sam was virtually quoting from his masterwork *Words on Wonder* that had a Foreword by my other friend, Doug Henning.

BEN ROBINSON VISITING THE SHARPE FAMILY IN 1986
SAM SHARPE IS ON THE LEFT.

If you care about the Art of Magic, you should study performing magic, and know that tricks are akin to steps in a dance. You use many tricks to create the illusion of magic. While there are those who think exacting nomenclature is folly, I contend it isn't. The more you understand about what you are doing, the better magician you will be. The better shows you do, the greater the audience reaction. And finally, maybe, one-day Magic will be revered as a true art form by the general public.

Right now, it isn't and the reason is, most magicians have no idea of what magic is. Most have no idea what wonder is or how to go about inspiring it. Most simply, do not care. This must change.

S. H. Sharpe eloquently wrote in *Words on Wonder*, "So a conjurer succeeds or fails *as a conjurer* to the extent that he succeeds or fails in creating illusions in the minds of spectators. But he may succeed as a comedian doing tricks without really succeeding as a conjurer-magician." Unfortunately, most who are mindless and simply seek fame using a magician's performance as a medium to achieve fame (or some other goal) have sought to undermine any notion of *genuinely wonder-inspiring* performance. Comedians who use "tricks" as "filler" are not magicians.

One so-called comedy-magic team who achieved fame in the 1980's sought to beat up Doug Henning as a buffoon, while their performance was neither magical nor really funny. *The Wall Street Journal* remarked of this Off-Broadway malevolent bastion as "hoodwinking the audience into believing they had seen something original and striking, when in actuality the joke was on them. There was nothing on the stage but amateurish excuse for cynicism." Master Magician Milbourne Christopher referred to this crew as "menacing to the art of magic." Christopher was later criticized for being "out of step" with current morays. Does genuine wonderment ever go out of style? We would hope not.

Overall, largely because many of those who seek to practice magic lack originality and guts, they play Follow the Leader and ape this cynicism without understanding the larger implications. Lesser performers choose the easier road of making nasty fun of magic, rather than endeavoring to perpetrate agreeable illusion producing wonder. Consequently "poetic magic feeling" has fallen out of what so-called "magicians" do and what audiences expect of magicians at large. This is a tragedy.

People who call themselves "magicians" who beat up magicians (admittedly an easy target given the modern age) have no idea what the Art of Magic is. Period.

SAM SHARPE WITH UNPUBLISHED WORKS

STUDYING WONDER-MAKING

If you want to up your salary, then up your performance. Up your game—do not imitate someone who has had success. Have the balls to create your own methods, effects, and yes, success.

At a performance at the famed national landmark Montauk Manor at the very tip of Long Island, the film director Steven Spielberg once attended my performance. He watched my show on the lawn in the courtyard, as part of the hotel's "Children's Festival." He then inquired if he might speak to me as I packed my case to depart. I told him I had a few minutes!

Spielberg said very specifically, "I just watched your show. The whole thing. You communicated an entertainment message to young and old alike …and…uh, that's hard to do." He looked at me as if I should respond with how I'd done this. I simply said, "I've been doing this a long time. Thanks for coming by. I'm sure you are busy."

I'm a fan of his movies, believing his film *"ET"* one of the best fantasy films ever made. But, it's a film. It doesn't happen in the same time and space as an audience at my live performance. He wondered how I'd gotten my message through and made people forget about their dinner reservations or that hot sun beat down on them for forty-five minutes during my performance. This is not to parade my success. This is to show the power of wonder working.

When wonder is incited, audiences become "spellbound." It is possible.

Magic is a form of visual poetry that provides hope through wonder.

Study that sentence and you will be a better magician. Know that a work of art is to be judged not by technical difficulties, but by the feelings and imagination it evokes. That is the true final lesson.

Rudolf Steiner wrote, "Human knowledge begins with wonder." It's a broad conceit, but look at any baby learning and see through their eyes—you'll get it. If magicians embraced this notion, the Art of Magic would be sacred. The Art of Magic would be respected as other arts are respected.

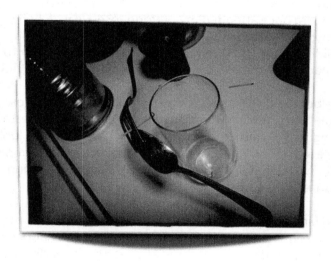

CREATING WONDER WITH EVERYDAY OBJECTS

THE IMPORTANCE OF WONDER

On Valentine's Day 2001, I was called to perform at the Center for Special Studies at the Cornell-Weill New York Presbyterian Medical Center. It is a highly isolated area of the hospital that cares for some of the oldest known HIV cases on the planet. Their Program Director Jenny Lytton brought me in as a "special guest" with one goal in mind—to reverse a threatening situation. AIDS patients take medications that are being tested; some that make them physically sick, but medicine that may prolong their life. It is difficult to get these patients to adhere to constant regimens that make them physically ill. The doctors were wary of Ms. Lytton's attempt to "break the paradigm." Valentine's Day was the hook magic was hung on as a present to the patients.

I worked in the receiving room at the clinic. Ms. Lytton wrote to me later that year:

"Dear Ben,

Thank you for the work you have done for our program. Your contributions to the Center for Special Studies have made a great difference to the patients and providers in our program as an HIV/AIDS care provider, exclusively serving indigent patients struggling with many obstacles to good health, your contribution as a magician has been innovative and unusual for us.

For the patients, your imagination and inspiring message that even the impossible can become possible, was a great gift to the mental health of the patients who have been able to enjoy your presence. You assisted us in our mission to make our clinic a welcoming and comfortable and unusual environment which is invaluable. If people feel intimidated or unwelcome, they will not seek care for themselves. Not only were you an inviting presence, but an entertaining one as well.

Your innovative ideas about the contributions of a magician's perspective to the medical community were also inspiring to the staff here. How better to understand people's perspectives and the way they interpret messages are invaluable lessons and tools for medical providers."

Similarly, my friend, the Grand Prix-winning World Champion Magician Johnny Ace Palmer was introduced to a boy sitting in a wheelchair. His small face was paralyzed since birth. He was unable to move his mouth, eyebrows and needed enormous assistance to do the most basic things.

Johnny is one of the most accomplished sleight of hand artists in the world. He approached the boy, whose condition remained atrophied for year and showed him something rare.

Johnny took a gleaming copper penny and showed his hand empty. His sleeve was rolled to the elbow. The boy looked at my friend as he tossed the copper penny skyward.

When the penny descended to Johnny's hand, the copper penny had changed during flight into a shining silver dime!

The boy, whose face was paralyzed since birth … broke into a huge smile!

Doctors came running, exclaiming loudly, their consternation completely confounded "What did you do? He's never moved! Wha…!!!"

The boy reached for the dime, and Johnny gave it to him.

Pandemonium.

No one could believe it. Nurses shed tears. Now it was the doctor's turn to have stone faces. Were the words not over-used…it was *real magic*.

It was because the boy felt *wonder*.

Wonder is important.

BEN ROBINSON WITH JOHNNY ACE PALMER

To conclude, I leave you in the hands of none other than Albert Einstein. Dr. Einstein wrote in his 1934 book *The World as I See It:*

The most beautiful experience we can have is the mysterious. It is the fundamental emotion which stands at the cradle of true art and science. Whoever does not know it and can no longer wonder, no longer marvel, is as good as dead, and his eyes are dimmed.

BEN ROBINSON — RING KING
PHOTO: KEVIN THOMASSON

AFTERWORD:
BEHIND BUDDHIST B°Y & BUBBLE

I am proud of many things in my professional life. Having traveled in over 20 countries with 6 different one-man shows, and having given over 10,000 performances to a rough estimate of three-million people, I am very grateful to have spent 40-years as a full time, traveling magician.

However, the photograph adorning the cover of this small book is truly among the things I consider to have been a special highpoint in my travels. It is my hope that knowing this may keep your attention for the next several minutes.

People who really know me well always remark that I am "a highly moral person." When I first heard this, I hadn't considered that about myself at all. But, now, after repeatedly having others say this to me, I agree. I told a client on the phone the other day, someone I had never before spoken to: "I am unimpressed by celebrity, fame, money or how big a house one has. I *am* impressed by kindness, morals, ethics, talent, and above all, selflessness." She responded, "You're hired."

Now, what is "moral" for one may not be "moral" for another; I realize that. Did Dr. Jekyll really find the actions of his counterpart Mr. Edward Hyde moral? What was moral when Robert Louis Stevenson wrote (at only age thirty-six), *The Strange Case of Dr. Jekyll and Mr. Hyde* in 1886 is now still pretty much the case.

The "Ripper" murders in Whitechapel, London, England succeeded Stevenson's novella by just 16-months. The surgically dissected prostitutes, and murdered victims, did create a sense of "dark wonder" when several similarities between the murdering psychopath of those prostitutes (who was *never* caught), and Stevenson's fictional tale were compared. Was life imitating art? Or did Stevenson exhibit prescience? To wonder: *not* knowing with a sense of excitement.

Dark wonder is really just hackneyed curiosity akin to visual gossip; it sells newspapers. Houdini said, in 1924, to his ghostwriter Walter B. Gibson, who then quoted it verbatim to me: "People do not like to see another person killed, but they like to be nearby." Whether it is the Whitechapel murders or the modern Phil Spector murder trial, those not involved, wonder. We do not know. We want to know, but we are confronted with the unknown. The unknown is integral to the enigmatic overall state of being.

Genuine, brilliant, energizing wonder is primary to life itself. A baby is born. Your team wins, when previously, in the last few minutes before the buzzer they were assured to lose! A marriage where love is in the air! And finally, but not least of all, when a magician does something genuinely amazing, thrilling, charming — *wondrous*! The previously destroyed bank note that winds up miraculously whole and untouched *inside* a sealed, fresh lemon! A miracle. To begin with, a bill inside a lemon has the overtones of surrealism. The two do not conform to any known reality. Bills do not grow inside lemons. But, in the magician's universe, the two somehow conclude a delightful, small, irrational play of death and resurrection.

Both Cardini and Doug Henning exhibited true awe at manifestations they were involved in, perhaps even commandeered, but nevertheless, the beauty of raw wonder enveloped them. Their performance involving this delightful human display transmitted to the audience. In fact, historians and theorists conclude that while Cardini's raw manual skill was exceptional, his acting ability was what put his act over, from variety halls to a command performance for King George V and later in life aboard ocean liners. Doug Henning verily revived magic as an art form, putting in motion what is now called The Henning Revolution, some 50 years later.

The photo that adorns this cover is untouched by modern technology. I shot this photo, amidst many others, on May 29, 1989 at Tengboche Monastery (approx. 14, 600 ft.), in The Khumbu valley, the Himalaya, Nepal. Those end credits denote perhaps the most famous monastery in the Himalaya, which I visited on my descent from Mount Everest, after six long weeks of walking, altitude sickness and sore muscles.

I had been invited by a Texan entrepreneur named Richard D. Bass, who, at the time was the oldest man to summit the roof of the world. (His climbing partner was Frank Wells, who later became the Chairman of the Walt Disney Company, and died in 1994 in a heli-skiing accident in the US. Frank and Dick's extraordinary true story is told in the Rick Ridgeway-penned book *Seven Summits*.)

My job, during the 150-mile trek was to entertain each night at dinner before all retired as the temperature sank below zero. Because magic doesn't need language to be appreciated, I provided a focul-point for climbers, trekkers, monks, and other adventurers. One night I made a champagne bottle disappear instantly. Then I had a man select a small cigarette paper, tear it into four pieces, and then have the torn papers magically restore to one whole piece in his hands. An Australian climber from another team we'd met earlier that day, remarked loudly to great laughter, "This bloke knows how to travel, champagne and rolling papers!" Yah, this bloke does know how to travel...

I know the language of wonder and it has been my constant travel companion, seeing me through more than one life-threatening situation.

Buddhist Boy & Bubble was shot accidentally. I'd taught Sherpas and others to make glycerin-based large soap bubbles. This happened during one of my last performances of the long trip. I'd saved my bubbles until the finish, wanting to fill a quarter-mile area with thousands of bubbles, smiles and laughter. It worked and I left to retire to my moldy tent, victim of the monsoon rains. I was trying to meditate amidst my raging headache from the altitude.

One of Tenzing Norgay's (the Sherpa who summited Mt. Everest with Sir Edmund Hillary in 1953) sons was a guide we'd encountered throughout our trip. His name is Tashi; a clever, England-educated charmer who speaks many languages. Tashi blew the bubbles you see in the front piece. It is his arm also extending into the photo. The boy was three, and I don't know his name, but I do know how he came to be at Tengboche. He was born to a Sherpa family, that was unable to raise him, and left to the monks for their expert care. This is common in this area of the world.

The lad ran around squealing in delight, chasing bubbles; jumping to pop them, constantly asking for more! He was as exciting as the bubbles to all of us! I missed most of this until my dear friend, Seattle-lawyer Jim Hammond, ducked his head inside my tent and said, "Ben you ought to grab your camera and join us. A lot of good karma you're creating out here." I told Jim that I was tired, had done my duty and would pass. Just then, The Boy ran passed the small tent entrance and I realized what Jim was saying. I grabbed my camera and was one foot out of the tent when I hit my weary head on the cross bar separating inside from outside. The jolt made me hit the shutter. The photograph, now owned (with full rights) by The American Himalayan Foundation based in San Francisco, of *Buddhist Boy & Bubble* is the result of that jolt.

I planned to go half way around the world and ascend to the Base Camp of mighty Chomolungma (translated from the

Tibetan "Mother Goddess of Us All" known to Westerners as Mount Everest). The Base Camp is where Everest begins at 18,000 feet. I wanted Everest as my backdrop as I conjured for The American Everest Team and others. People from nine countries speaking at least twelve languages saw that show. Maybe twenty-five saw what happened in the yak-grazing fields of Tengboche that fateful day in May, 1989. My hope is that you look at this photograph and realize why I did what I did. It is all there in the face of the boy discovering a soap bubble for the very first time.

I believe wonder is our natural state of being. I think we need wonder to survive as a species. Wonder is timeless, provides hope — it's important. Wonder is the basis of all art and science Professor Einstein tells us.

I sincerely believe that if we all live with a sense of wonder in our lives; our lives will be filled with joy. Doug Henning said that repeatedly throughout his professional career, and I agree with him. The photograph Buddhist Boy & Bubble shows and reminds us of wonder. It may even create wonder.

If you have never felt wonder, I hope you seek the genuinely wondrous in life.

If you have felt wonder; I hope you share that feeling with others.

The world needs true wonder now—more than ever.

—Ben Robinson
New York City
November 23, 2014
Harpo Marx's birthday

W°NDER GH°ST

Sit facing the person you will amaze, knees almost touching. Now, take your fingers and hold them in front of the other person's eyes, and extend your index fingers as if you were pointing your right finger to his or her left eye, and your left index finger to their right eye.

Explain that you will summon a ghost.

Tell your partner to gently close his eyes, and when he does, place your forefingers very gently on his closed eyelids. Suddenly! Your partner feels a sharp thump on his left shoulder. The ghost has made its appearance. Your partner may be slightly alarmed, but should not at that moment under any circumstances immediately open their eyes with our fingers touching the eyelids! (Explain this beforehand.)

If they're playing along, they will feel amazement that with your two hands on their eyelids, and no one possibly behind them, it felt to them as if you grew a third arm and whacked them on the back.

Okay, Mulder, so what really happened?

Simple, Scully. When your partner closed his eyes, you extend your left middle finger as well, as if making a horizontal peace sign. That way you can carefully touch both eyes with two fingers of your left hand, freeing one hand to deliver the unsettling clap on the partner's left shoulder. The finger switch takes a bit of timing and practice.

Your haunted partner will immediately look behind themselves for your non-existent confederate. So be sure to return your right arms with your finger extended and your left arm with your forefinger extended before they open their eyes. And don't give up the ghost to your friend, or you'll ruin a nice little 19th century mystery.

(Reprinted from *Connecticut College Magazine,* Fall, 2002. Used by Permission.)

FURTHER SUGGESTED READING

The following books have been written by venerable sources — who knew what they were talking about. All of the titles bring many different perspectives to the pursuit of presenting magic as an artful entertainment that enhances the feeling of wonder and joyful expansion of consciousness.

Gibson, Walter B., *THE MASTER MAGICIANS*, Doubleday & Co., Garden City, NY 1966.

Harrison, John., SPELLBOUND: THE WONDER-FILLED LIFE OF DOUG HENNING, Box Office Books, 2009.

Howard, Max., *CREATING THEATRICAL MAGIC*, Theory and Art of Magic Press, 2014.

Maskelyne, Nevil., Devant, David, *OUR MAGIC*, Edited by Paul Fleming, Lee Jacobs Reproductions, Ohio, 1992.

Nelms, Henning., *MAGIC & SHOWMANSHIP*, Dover Publications, New York, 1969.

Ortiz, Darwin., *STRONG MAGIC*, Kaufman & Company, 1994.

Sharpe, Sam H., *NEO-MAGIC — The Art of The Conjurer*, George Johnson Magical Publications, London, 1946.

Sharpe, Sam H., *WORDS ON WONDER*, Wonder Publications, US, 1984.

Taylor, Rogan., *THE DEATH AND RESURRECTION SHOW*, Anthony Blond Pub., London, 1995.

Weber, Ken., *MAXIMUM ENTERTAINMENT*, Ken Weber Productions, Lake Success, NY, 2003.

THE AUTHOR

Ben Robinson started in magic in 1968. He became a professional magician in 1974. He's authored *Twelve Have Died* (1986), *The MagiClAn: John Mulholland' Secret Life* (2008), and *Magic & The Silent Clowns* (2011) among others. He has been a regular contributor to *VANISH* since issue #1. In 2014 he was made Contributing Editor. He's given over 10,000 performances of 6 different one–man shows in 22 countries; entertaining over 3-million people live. He's made a live Easter Bunny appear for critically ill children at NY Presbyterian Hospital, cured clinical depression in some of the oldest known HIV cases, caught rifle-fired bullets in his teeth at Niagara Falls and Houdini's grave, and is the first magician in history to make diamond-studded rings appear on all of his fingers. *The New York Times* wrote: "Ben Robinson is an internationally acclaimed Master Magician."

His current-show *MysteriuM* sold-out its debut engagement at The Suffolk Theatre in Riverhead, NY on Houdini's birthday, April 6, 2013. World Champion Magician Johnny Ace Palmer partnered with Ben Robinson on a two man bill and played to capacity audiences in the Parlour of Prestidigitation at Hollywood's world famous Magic Castle in both June of 2010 and 2011. Robinson was reviewed as "comedy magic at its finest." Mr. Palmer said to Ben Robinson after the shows, "You are the coolest magician I know. Actually, that doesn't even begin to describe you!"

Among his favorite memories are: conjuring for the American Everest Team at the Base Camp (17,800 ft.) of Mt. Everest in Nepal in 1989, and appearing before Frank Sinatra, Sir Edmund Hillary, Groucho Marx, Diane Keaton and HRH Princess Anne of England among an estimated three million others since his first performance on December 15, 1974.

Ben Robinson has lived in New York City for 38 years. He and his wife An, are owned by their ever-young rascally rascal parrot — Stubby.

See: illusiongenius.com

ALSO BY BEN ROBINSON

Writing & Recording:

Magic & The Silent Clowns	(2011)
The John Booth Reader	(2010)
The MagiCIAn: John Mulholland's Secret Life	(2008)
The Situation of Magic in the 21st Century	(2003)
Secrets of a Professional Magician	(2001)
Ben Robinson on Synchronicity	(2001)
The John Booth Index	(1990)
Mouth Coil Magic	(1987)
Twelve Have Died	(1986)
Indian Magic	(1982)

One Man Shows:

MysteriuM	(2011)
L'Art De La Magie	(2009)
Time For Magic	(2007)
Pyschodyssey	(1991-1993)
After Magic?	(1989)
Out Of Order	(1988)

Made in the USA
Middletown, DE
10 December 2021